A STEP-BY-STEP BOOK ABOUT
GUPPIES

JACK C. HARRIS

Photography:
Dr. Herbert R. Axelrod; Frickhinger; Dr. W. Foerster; Michael Gilroy; Dr. Harry Grier, courtesy Florida Tropical Fish Farmers Association; T. J. Horeman; Dr. Karl Knaack; Dr. F. Myers; H. J. Richter; Mervin F. Roberts; Stan Shubel; Mitsuyoshi Tatematsu, courtesy Midori Shobo, Fish Magazine, Japan; Ruda Zukal.

Humorous illustrations by Andrew Prendimano.

Dedication
To Kelly

Distributed in the UNITED STATES by T.F.H. Publications, Inc., One T.F.H. Plaza, Neptune City, NJ 07753; in CANADA to the Pet Trade by H & L Pet Supplies Inc., 27 Kingston Crescent, Kitchener, Ontario N2B 2T6; Rolf C. Hagen Ltd., 3225 Sartelon Street, Montreal 382 Quebec; in CANADA to the Book Trade by Macmillan of Canada (A Division of Canada Publishing Corporation), 164 Commander Boulevard, Agincourt, Ontario M1S 3C7; in ENGLAND by T.F.H. Publications Limited, Cliveden House/Priors Way/Bray, Maidenhead, Berkshire SL6 2HP, England; in AUSTRALIA AND THE SOUTH PACIFIC by T.F.H. (Australia) Pty. Ltd., Box 149, Brookvale 2100 N.S.W., Australia; in NEW ZEALAND by Ross Haines & Son, Ltd., 18 Monmouth Street, Grey Lynn, Auckland 2, New Zealand; in SINGAPORE AND MALAYSIA by MPH Distributors (S) Pte., Ltd., 601 Sims Drive, #03/07/21, Singapore 1438; in the PHILIPPINES by Bio-Research, 5 Lippay Street, San Lorenzo Village, Makati Rizal; in SOUTH AFRICA by Multipet Pty. Ltd., 30 Turners Avenue, Durban 4001. Published by T.F.H. Publications, Inc. Manufactured in the United States of America by T.F.H. Publications, Inc.

CONTENTS

Introduction

After the Goldfish, the Guppy is considered the most popular fish kept in home aquariums around the world. The beauty of these tiny fish, the ease of care and breeding as well as the small price you have to pay for one or more of them all contribute to their popularity. Their general hardiness and their fascinating natural habits are also major factors which account for their ever increasing prevalence in the world's aquariums.

Many experts consider the Guppy the "universal" pet fish, having qualities which appeal to everyone from the beginning fish keeper to the professional fish breeder. The beginners see the Guppy as a colorful addition to their aquariums, while the breeder sees the small fish as a ripe subject for selective breeding which has already resulted in a fantastically diverse array of beautiful Guppies. In some quarters, it is also known as the "rainbow fish" and the "millions fish" because of its dazzling array of colors.

It is impossible to determine the original distribution of the Guppy, since these colorful fish are found today in so many warm climates of the Americas and in various other locations around the world. While their exotic beauty is one of the major reasons for their appearance worldwide, there are several environmental concerns that have resulted in their introduction into various regions. Guppies are, for instance, highly valued in the West Indies because they destroy the larvae of mosquitos that carry malaria. It is believed that their presence in those waters is due completely to their introduction by man to combat the insects. In fact, this has been the explanation for Guppies

FACING PAGE:
Male Guppies in a tastefully arranged aquarium display just a few of the different colors and shapes for which they're well known. Attractive, prolific and easy to care for, Guppies have delighted millions of tropical fish fanciers for many years.

being found in so many places. Originally, in nature, Guppies were found in the islands of the southern Caribbean Sea and as far south as southern Brazil.

Scientifically, the Guppy is described as a small, active, carnivorous, freshwater fish, *Poecilia reticulata,* belonging to the topminnow family Poeciliidae. It was named in honor of the Trinidadian ichthyologist R. J. Lechmere Guppy.

For many years, there was a great deal of confusion regarding the specific genus of the Guppy because of the great diversity in Guppy males. Johannes Schmidt, a Danish biologist known for his studies in eel migrations, and Olaf Winge were the first scientists to deal with the hereditary transmission of color in Guppies. Winge's 1927 paper described 18 genes for various caudal fin variations and color patterns of the Guppy. Hybridization experiments showed that even the Guppies in certain geographic areas with various color patterns, which were believed to be new species or new genera, were actually

The adult Guppies shown here are very close in coloration to the original wild-type Guppies; if anything, the male is even a little plainer than wild Guppies.

A far cry from what long-ago Guppy breeders experimented with as their initial breeding stock, this magnificent male evidences great improvement in both color and finnage development.

members of one species. Winge and Schmidt were responsible for the elimination of the profusion of scientific names for Guppies.

Many Guppy keepers are interested in breeding these fish because of the wide and beautiful color variations. There has been so much selective breeding among Guppies that there are few traceable characteristics of the original strain left. The original Guppy in the wild was considered an interesting specimen, but it was generations away from the beautiful and brilliantly colored Guppies seen today, with their long, flowing fins. They are, however, still the exact same fish as far as scientific classification is concerned. Scientists and professional fish breeders recognize this and realize that no matter how "fancy" a Guppy may be, or if it is regarded as a "Super Guppy" specimen, it still has the same taxonomic classifications as a common Guppy or a genetic reject.

It is the male Guppy which is often kept in aquariums because of its brilliant coloration. These color lines are the distant offshoots of the strains developed by British and European Guppy enthusiasts during their attempts to improve the breed

by selective breeding. Although advancements have gone far beyond these early attempts, varieties such as veiltails, scarftails, pintails, speartails, cofertails, and roundtails, top, bottom, and double swordtails were all created long ago.

Today, with the various color patterns having been explored to such degrees, breeders seem more interested in developing the tails of the Guppies. Some of the results have produced Guppy males with tails almost twice the length of their

The most popular of the fancy Guppy varieties on the market today are the veiltails and deltatails, in which the males' tails have been fanned out, with the angle formed by the joining of the upper and lower edges of the tail at the caudal peduncle being greater in the deltatails than in the veiltails. This fish is a deltatail, as its caudal angulation is closer to 60 degrees than to 45 degrees.

bodies. These beautiful tails fan out and are covered with dazzling colors and swish around and guide the fish on his darting swims around the aquarium.

The normal Guppy is about one inch long, tinted with combinations of yellow, red, orange, green, blue, and purple, and spotted with black. Just as no two snowflakes have the same crystal pattern, no two individual Guppies have the same pattern of color.

Introduction

Continual breeding attempts and the growth of interest in this aspect of the hobby of fish keeping resulted in organized Guppy-fancier groups being formed. These national groups created Guppy standards which breeders pay close attention to while continuing to improve the breed and create new color strains. More recently, breeders have been concentrating on attempts to create variations of finnage on Guppy breeds. Most of the experts in these fields regard the possibilities for endless variation as being wide open.

The most beautiful Guppies are the males. More often than not, the male of any given species of bird, mammal, or fish is much more brilliantly colored than its female counterpart. Nature tends to automatically protect females in the wild and seems to know that predators will notice a brighter color of fur, feathers, or fins and chase after the male as its prey. The males seem to understand this instinctively and will successfully use this quirk of nature to lead dangerous enemies away from the females and their young. The female Guppy, which is about 2 inches long, conforms to this by having a dull color, usually plain yellow-gray.

Even the females of fancy Guppy strains now have tail fins much expanded in size. This female Guppy's tail is not especially large in comparison to that of many other fancy females, but her tail color is exceptionally good.

Typical courtship behavior of Guppies, with the male posturing before the female.

While beauty and the fascination of breeding may be the major reasons for keeping Guppies, others keep the fish and let them breed on their own simply for quantity. A healthy pair of mating Guppies will produce a new litter every four weeks, the number of young varying from two to over 100 at a time. As many as five litters are produced as a result of a single mating. Prior to mating, male Guppies are seen spreading their fins before the female much in the manner of certain birds in an elaborate courtship ceremony.

Guppies are livebearers, giving birth to fish which were fully formed inside the female's body after fertilization. Breeding can be an exact science, so certain rules and precautions must be observed. For instance, the young, newly born Guppies are frequently devoured by the parents. In their native surroundings, they are able to survive by hiding in the vegetation which grows on the bottom of their waters. Guppy breeders raising new Guppies in aquariums are always careful to provide separate tanks or thick vegetation for the young to insure the safe segregation of the offspring from their parents or other fish.

Introduction

The particular habits of Guppies are another one of the reasons for their popularity. They dart and swim around in fascinating patterns that enhance their color variations. Unlike many similar fish, Guppies do not form shoals, or schools, but swim in seemingly random patterns, independent of one another. They will appear to form such shoals if alarmed by splashing or swirling water, but this is merely a simultaneous reaction to a disturbance in their environment. By nature, they don't travel together in the manner usually associated with fish of their size.

A baby Guppy being born. This baby still has a large yolk sac attached, characteristic of a newborn livebearing fish that has been born prematurely; the baby will not be able to swim normally until the yolk sac has been absorbed.

Keeping Guppies is a wonderful hobby. The color and the fascinating activities can provide hours of enjoyment for their keepers. Unfortunately, as is often the case with the common Goldfish, uninformed keepers often make mistakes and the fish die early deaths. This certainly need not happen, as many pet shop owners and professional fish breeders point out. If properly cared for, Guppies can live healthy lives over two years.

The beauty of Guppies has made them popular items of decor. Many interior decorators occasionally suggest to certain of their clients that they acquire an aquarium of Guppies to enhance the design of a given room. While experts often agree on the beautiful addition Guppies could make to any room, they urge owners to remember that these are *living* creatures and should be treated as such. If they are thought of only as items of decoration, then there is a danger that they could be *treated* merely as decorations. Such an attitude could be potentially fatal to the fish and should be discouraged.

There have also been some studies indicating that an aquarium of fish has a calming effect on hectic office atmospheres. Sociologists indicate that people in an office, reception room, or doctor's waiting room are calmed by the presence of a fish tank bubbling with activity and life.

Expert fish keepers also report the calming effect that their enthusiasm for the fish has had on them. However, they too stress the importance of treating the Guppies as living things rather than instruments for the use of surrounding workers or patients.

Keeping and even breeding Guppies can be educational and tremendously rewarding for children, but only with strict parental supervision. Additionally, parents should become as knowledgeable as possible about Guppy keeping before turning over the responsibility to children. Guppies are, for instance, hearty eaters. They thrive in aquarium water temperatures around 75° to 85°F. However, overfeeding, incorrect water temperatures, and other life-threatening situations can easily arise if children are left on their own to care for their pet Guppies.

It is often the case that people will consider fish "throwaway" pets, believing that they are short-lived and can be easily replaced. While the latter may be true, the former statement isn't. Even though pet fish may be easy to obtain, taking care of them is still a task which should be met with a firm sense of responsibility. After all, by having *any* pet in your home, you are taking on the charge of another life or lives. Such a commitment should not be taken lightly, even if you're talking about "just a fish."

Introduction

This sense of responsibility should be even more strongly expressed in the case of children. Many youngsters view all pet care the same way. If they see a lax attitude when caring for Guppies, they could very well equate it with the care of other, more conventional pets such as cats and dogs. Since these domesticated animals show a higher degree of intelligence and personality, any problems arising from lack of proper care have greater impact. Nevertheless, a comparable degree of responsible care should always be practiced so that children understand the necessity of extending such care to all living creatures. Beyond the biological lessons that can be learned from the care and breeding of Guppies, this sense of responsibility is, potentially, one of the most important.

Only if adults *and* children are educated as to the proper care and keeping of Guppies (or *any* pet for that matter) can the full enjoyment of Guppy keeping be realized. These beautiful pets will provide years of fascinating fish watching.

Whether the Guppies you purchase are the plainest of the plain or among the fanciest available, they deserve the best you can reasonably give them. Apart from the humane considerations involved, it simply makes good sense to give your fish good care.

Selecting Your Guppies

Many people want Guppies for their aquarium for the sole purpose of having some of the colorful fish to add beauty to their underwater environment. They have no initial desire to try and breed the animals. However, when choosing a Guppy or Guppies for your aquarium, it is a good idea to keep in mind the specifications for selecting good breeding stock. If you keep these ideas in mind, then you will have a better chance of selecting a Guppy that will be healthy and one which will provide enjoyment and beauty for a long time to come.

Breeders, or those fish keepers who are looking to start breeding, always want to begin with the best. The same should be true for a newcomer. Choosing the best fish you can find will ensure the longevity of the animal and, if you *do* decide to breed in the future, you'll be one step closer to your goal if you start out with the best Guppy or Guppies you can buy.

Begin at your local pet store, of course. Since Guppies breed rapidly and often, it is best to start out with one pair. If you begin with a multitude, you will have to consider such things as extra equipment and additional room to adequately house this large family. Your pet shop owner will aid you in selecting your Guppies and will be able to give you good advice on their care, feeding, and, if you are so inclined, their breeding.

Also ask your dealer to be certain of the sex of your fish. For instance, it is not good practice to house one female

FACING PAGE:
These male Guppies represent just a few of the many different color and tail varieties available. There is no one "best" variety; a hobbyist's choice is purely a matter of personal taste.

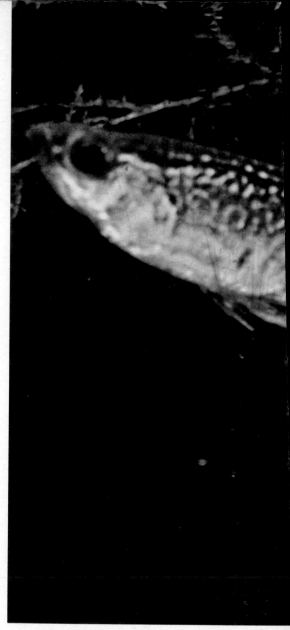

This yellow snakeskin male wouldn't be up for any awards at a Guppy show, but he's pleasingly colorful nevertheless. Snakeskins are one of the more popular varieties.

with a pair of males. Two males will constantly harass a single female—a very unhealthy situation for all fish involved.

The females are normally twice as long as the males. The female's body should have good depth and be well-rounded. Breeders take special note of any color markings that show up on the female. Any such colors beyond their normal

yellow-gray coloring may indicate color characteristics that will show up in future offspring.

You should also be sure that your fish is sturdy. You can determine this by careful examination while it darts around the pet store tank. Also look for a good body shape which is well-developed. Make certain its tail allows it to swim in a nor-

mal, natural fashion. Often, some selectively bred Guppies have caudal fins which are developed to such a degree that they force the Guppy to swim in a peculiar and erratic manner. A well-formed caudal fin should angle away from the Guppy's body and, on a male, can actually be about the same length as its body.

Since Guppies are rather independent swimmers, not traveling in "schools," it is usually easy to spot and observe closely a single one for a time before making your selection—a distinct advantage for a newcomer.

Take this time to make a special note of the color. First, it should be a shade or tone you find pleasing. Second, a healthy Guppy's colors should be vibrant and sharp.

All of these characteristics can be checked if the potential owner has "done his homework" by reading and studying books on Guppies available at the library or the local pet shop. By familiarizing yourself with the best qualities of the various types of Guppies, you will be able to spot deformities or abnormalities on a fish. Avoid these types since they are often more susceptible to diseases than sturdy, well-formed Guppies.

Additionally, before selecting your pet Guppies, you should also become familiar with the symptoms of the more common diseases that attack Guppies. Armed with this infor-

The intensity of a Guppy's coloring can be even more important than the color's extent in determining how well a given individual conforms to the standard for its type.

This male swordtail Guppy is very short on finnage in contrast to his veiltail and deltatail relatives, but he has crisp, colorful markings. Swordtail Guppies are more popular in Europe than in the United States and the Far East.

mation, you will be able to spot a sick Guppy easily.

Naturally, pet shop owners are acutely aware of the dangers of disease and are always on the lookout for unhealthy stock. However, with the multitude of fish they must oversee every day, there is always a chance that something unforeseen will slip by. Educated shoppers will be helpful to themselves, the shop owners, and the pets.

Remember that you are selecting not only a pet but also everything that is needed to keep that pet alive and healthy. Make certain you learn as much as you can about your Guppy's basic food and aquarium needs before you buy it. All of these have to be established before you bring your fish home. Your pet shop owner will aid you in creating an environment for your new pets so that they will remain healthy and contented and bring you years of pleasure and educational fun.

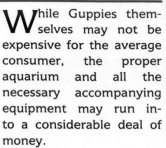

While Guppies themselves may not be expensive for the average consumer, the proper aquarium and all the necessary accompanying equipment may run into to a considerable deal of money.

Housing Your Guppies

However, if you shop around to as many good pet stores in your immediate area as possible, you will be able to find the best prices for the materials and equipment you need to provide a safe and healthy home for your Guppies. Good pet shop owners will be more than willing to help you select your guppy as well as the proper materials for a safe environment.

There are a great number of instructive texts concerning the proper setting up of an aquarium. Our aim in this volume is to offer a working knowledge of the proper way to house your fish so that the reader can make an intelligent purchase. Once you know the proper equipment to look for and the right questions to ask, then looking for a home for your guppies will not only be easier but also less expensive.

The first thing you will need is a fish tank. If this is your first experience at keeping fish, the best size should be a tank with a 20 to 30 gallon capacity. Aquariums are available in a wide variety of shapes and sizes, although the rectangular ones are by far the most popular. All the experts appear to agree that an aquarium constructed of all glass equipped with a plastic top (and sometimes a plastic bottom) is your best bet. Your primary concern should be for your Guppies. Fish breathe by using the oxygen dissolved in the water. Oxygen can enter the water through aeration or by simple exposure to the air at the surface. Generally, the more surface area exposed to the

FACING PAGE:
Male Guppies representing different tail types and color varieties. Regardless of type, all Guppies must have certain basic needs fulfilled in order for them to develop properly and look good.

air, the more oxygen there is in the water. This is why long and narrow tanks are more popular than tall ones. It is also the reason most experts urge you to stay away from bowls. These bowls, usually identified more with goldfish than with Guppies, are always extremely narrow at the top, providing little air.

The basic formula for fish survival in tanks is one which allows for 20 square inches of water surface for each body inch of fish, measuring from the point where the tail meets the body to the mouth.

You should resist the inclination to buy your fish, buy your tank, rush home, fill it with water and start watching. Instead, the wiser fish enthusiast sets up his aquarium completely before buying his fish.

The first thing you must do once you bring your aquarium tank home is to make certain it does not leak. The only way to determine this is to fill it with water and check it carefully for leaks. Even the costliest aquariums can spring leaks. The seams are carefully sealed, but rough handling or even the slightest bump can cause one or more of these seals to be broken.

Set your tank in a safe place and fill it with water of the same temperature as it will be when your Guppies are placed inside. Some experts spread dark colored blotting paper underneath the tank so that any leaks will show up easily. If your tank is brand new and you discover leaks, your pet shop owner will usually replace it for you. However, be sure that a replacement offer is made prior to testing for leaks yourself. Many pet shop owners will test the tank right in their shop before you take it home. Still, during the trip home there might be seal breakage, so it's best to test it again.

Once you've determined that your tank is watertight, you should decide where it will rest. A filled aquarium is very heavy and cannot be moved easily. Emptying it and changing its location are difficult and sometimes messy tasks. Once it's placed, it should remain at that location. For this reason, you should decide *exactly* where you intend to place your guppy tank before you go to the shop to make your purchase.

First of all, avoid direct sunlight. The rays of the sun on the sides of your glass tank will only encourage the growth

of the microscopic plants known as algae. It does not take too long for algae growth to completely cover the sides of an aquarium and totally hide your view of your colorful new Guppies. Your aquarium should be placed in a room that is as dust-free as possible. Tobacco and paint fumes can also have bad effects on aquarium water and may be potentially harmful to your Guppies. For instance, never place your aquarium in a freshly painted room.

Take your time in making your selection from among the different types of Guppies available. You can't operate a selective breeding program sensibly if you keep switching from one variety to another. The male Guppies shown here, for example, all exhibit individual qualities that have to be bred for systematically if they are to be produced with consistency.

Some novice fish keepers question the need for keeping the aquarium clean. They point to streams, rivers, and ponds in nature which, even though polluted, have healthy Guppies swimming happily around in them. In reality, the outdoor bodies of water are subject to great aeration as well as a certain amount of natural cleansing despite today's pollution problems. Such is not the case with indoor aquariums. You have to make sure your Guppies are in a safe, healthy environment if you want them to live reasonably healthy and lengthy lives.

It should be obvious that your pet shop owner would be particularly knowledgeable about artificial light for aquariums. Over 90% of the fish in pet shops are kept under the rays of artificial light. Such illumination is also excellent if you want to show off your Guppies' beauty during the evening hours. After all, though care for the fish themselves should *never* be minimized, it is recognized that in many cases Guppies are kept for their *beauty.* Artificial light, if properly used, is one of the best ways to exhibit this beauty. If artificial lighting is what you desire, you will have to have a reflector for your aquarium. Luck-

Undergravel filters can be hidden almost completely; they use the gravel substrate of an aquarium as the filter medium in which organic waste is trapped.

Filtration of an aquarium does more than just keep the aquarium free of suspended debris. It also provides helpful aeration and water movement. Power filters such as those shown here are very efficient at aerating an aquarium as well as filtering it.

ily, most aquarium manufacturers include these reflectors with all the electrical connections and sockets needed for the installation of a fluorescent light bulb. This reflected fluorescent light gives off very little heat, only slightly changing the water temperature. This is why fluorescent light is the most popular artificial illumination for Guppies and other aquarium fish. Incandescent lights are used in some cases, but these have a tendency to heat up the water too much (a rise of 10°F is not uncommon) and will increase the algae growth which may be harmful to your Guppies.

Most temperature problems can be controlled by the use of an aquarium heater and thermostat. Many varieties of such aquarium heaters and thermostats are available at your local pet stores. The size of the heater you select should be directly in proportion to the size of your tank.

Maintaining a proper temperature is important. Guppies do best in water between 75° and 80°F but *gradual* fluctua-

tions of 5° either up or down should not cause any serious damage. However, if you have to transfer fish from one aquarium to another, it is always wise to make a careful check of the temperature and DH and pH levels to make sure there are no drastic differences. This is especially important when transferring newly hatched fry.

Fortunately, the pH level of the water is not as critical a concern with Guppies as it is with other fish varieties as long as the levels are in a 6.6 to 7.6 range and consistent. The DH (or carbonate hardness or water hardness) should be kept around 4° to 6°, which is approximately 70 to 105 p.p.m. This will keep the water somewhere below hard, per se, but it is not considered soft either. The pH may change frequently, but only slightly, and this is not dangerous. Your pet shop stocks kits for testing pH. Some brands are strictly testing kits while others actually include the needed chemicals to alter the pH levels of your aquarium water.

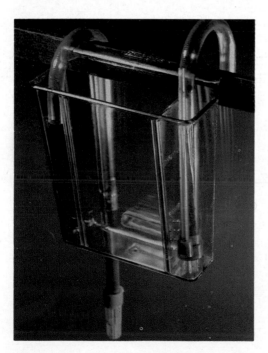

Like many of the power filters this filter also hangs on the side of the tank and works by siphoning water from the tank into the filter compartment, where it is filtered through a porous absorbent substance before being returned to the tank. This filter, however, is not a power filter and must be operated by an air pump.

Housing

Most aquariums utilize a filter. These are available in a wide assortment, all of which are found at your local pet store. They work by cycling the water continually through activated charcoal and additional filtering agents. Some are hung on the sides of the tank, while others are actually hidden underneath gravel. Your pet shop owner will help you in selecting the kind you will need.

Normally, your regular maintenance routine should require you to partially change the water about once every two weeks. You should change only about one-quarter to one-third of the total water each time and wait at least a full 24 hours between any changes. It is not necessary to dechlorinate for a change this small.

Of course, over a period of a couple of weeks, depending on your Guppy population, a certain amount of unsightly

Vibrator pumps are the most popular of air pumps. They are available in many different styles and ranges of power and are designed to give years of trouble-free performance.

waste and debris settles on the bottom of your aquarium, soiling the gravel and the tank in general. This waste has the potential to cause problems if it is not removed regularly. Bacteria can easily breed under these conditions and disease can begin to spread.

It is extremely important to clean the gravel before placing it in your aquarium—even the kinds which are commercially cleaned and available from your pet shop. Using a flow of warm water, stir the gravel in a bucket until the water running off is free of sediment. If you are using natural gravel, make sure there are no sharp edges that could possibly harm your fish.

Unlike many other species of fish, Guppies don't actually require aquatic plants in their environment for survival. Many thrive without them at all. However, most novices and experts alike feel that an aquarium without plant life lacks much of the beauty associated with keeping fish. Breeders recognize the importance of plant life as hiding places for newly hatched Guppy fry since improperly fed parents often eat the young . . . if they can *find* them.

Like plants, gravel on the bottom of your tank isn't really *necessary* either. Again, it is suggested for the sheer beauty of your aquarium. Some experts suggest that if you do not desire a gravel-covered aquarium bottom, it might be possible to

Provided with proper illumination and allowed to grow densely, even the so-called "tape grasses" like *Vallisneria* can form shelters for the fish.

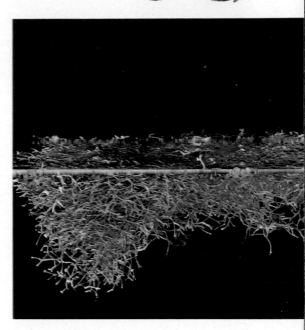

Riccia needs good lighting in order to proliferate, but once it starts growing well it forms a thick vegetative mat at the top of the aquarium and is difficult to penetrate by adult fish chasing babies.

have your plants growing in compost contained in ceramic containers where needed. This is a possible alternative, but the gravel-covered bottom is usually the more desirable.

Personal preference should determine the variety of plant life for your aquarium. However, many experts feel that watersprite *(Ceratopteris thalicroides)* helps to maintain the best water conditions for Guppies. One of the reasons for the popularity of watersprite for Guppy aquariums is that this particular plant enhances the colors of the Guppy more vividly. Others feel that any of the *Sagittaria* or *Vallisneria* plant species are equally suitable as well. Floating plants are good ideas for inclusion in aquariums where females are to deliver their young. These large masses can protect the young from cannibalistic females. Varieties include crystalwort *(Riccia fluitans)* and hornwort *(Ceratophyllum demersum)*. If your Guppies are properly fed, there is little danger of a mother devouring her young. However, since this *is* a common problem, you should separate newly born fry from their mother as soon as possible after birth.

Siphons, dip tubes and other debris-removing accessories are handy items to have around, as they help keep the aquarium clean.

As with gravel and compost, plants should be cleaned before they are introduced into your water. Your local pet shop stocks special plant sterilizing solutions manufactured expressly for this purpose.

You should keep a regular schedule for cleaning your aquarium. Fortunately, this is not a difficult task. Aquarium manufacturers and pet shop owners have been encountering cleaning problems for years. Their accumulated knowledge has provided a wide variety of solutions to the problems of keeping your aquarium clean and healthy.

Accumulation of dirt, mulm, and other waste begins to make your tanks unsightly. You can use a 5-foot siphon tube to drain off a portion of the dirt into a bucket and replace an equal amount of the water you removed. Make sure that the replacement water is the same temperature as the water in the tanks. You must do all you can to make sure your Guppies don't have a stressful reaction to a drastic temperature change, up or down. Either one is dangerous even to Guppies, who are

Housing

known for being able to survive in a variety of water temperatures. Be sure that none of your fish get too close to the end of the siphoning tube too since the suction force is potentially dangerous. These periodic partial water changes and a population of certain scavengers will help you to keep your Guppies' home healthy.

Remember that the best way to provide a safe beginning home for your Guppies is to have the aquarium already prepared before you bring your fish home. Pet shop owners have many ways for you to transport your fish. One of the most popular ways is to place the fish in a small plastic bag filled with water from the shop aquarium where they had been kept. It is extremely important that you take your fish home and put them in the already-prepared tank as soon as possible. The oxygen content of a sealed plastic bag can be depleted very rapidly, even with a single Guppy. If you have more than one swimming around in the little bag, then the oxygen supply will be used up even faster.

Two different types of breeding "traps" used for saving the babies of livebearing species. Pet shops offer many different baby-saving devices.

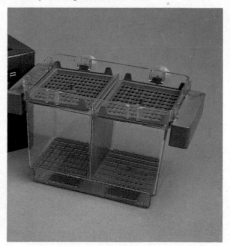

Normally, if you are going to be away for an extended period, you should clean your tank, making partial water changes and any other periodic maintenance duties before you're scheduled to leave. This way, all anyone has to do in your absence is feed your fish. Some of the commercial feeders can be rigged to dispense food at regular intervals. This could be the answer to your problem if you are going to be away for a short time.

If you are breeding Guppies, your problems for being away are (if you'll pardon the pun) multiplied. In this case, you would need an assistant who is as committed as you are in regard to the breeding of your Guppies. Fortunately, the fascination of Guppy breeding is one that is easily shared. Finding

Snails are the most common scavengers used in an aquarium housing Guppies. They might actually manufacture more dirt than they remove, but they're interesting to watch. The snail shown is one of the *Ampullaria* species, generally sold as "mystery" snails.

Today's aquarium remedies and preventives are very effective, but they are not to be used indiscriminately; check with your pet dealer for recommendations about specific treatments.

someone who is willing and eager to keep records, carefully observe, and otherwise aid you in such projects should be as rewarding as the actual hobby. If you make sure they are fed properly, keep their aquariums as clean as possible and become educated towards recognizing diseases in their earliest stages, you will have a healthy, thriving population of Guppies for many years to come. If you are successful in all of these areas, you will help put an end to the myth that Guppies and other varieties of pet fish are short-lived. With proper care, all fish can survive much longer than is commonly believed.

Kits for measuring the relative acidity/alkalinity of the water in an aquarium can be useful in providing a valuable warning to the aquarist if the water is at an extreme pH value.

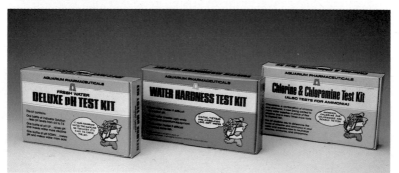

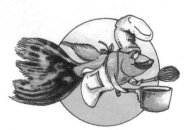

Feeding & Health

Feeding your Guppies properly is your first concern regarding the health of your fish. Luckily, Guppies are particularly easy to feed since they are satisfied with just about any conventional diet. They are hardy eaters with huge appetites. They will happily consume any kind of dry fish food and eat their fill. However, the novice fishkeeper must be warned that dry fishfoods are not enough to keep their Guppies healthy. Dry diets should be supplemented with other varieties of food, such as freeze-dried, frozen or live. Worms are good, especially if you obtain a worm feeder from your local pet shop. Such feeding devices help to keep your aquarium cleaner. Tubifex worms, for instance, are also an excellent supplement, as are mosquito larvae, which Guppies are so well-known for devouring. You should consult your pet shop owner about the availability of varieties of live foods.

A newly hatched Guppy fry thrives best on newly hatched brine shrimp. Frozen adult brine shrimp is considered one of the best frozen varieties of fishfood for Guppies of any age.

Those interested in breeding Guppies on a competition level should be aware that experts agree on feeding the young, growing Guppies as often as possible. Some breeders actually supply up to six mealtimes in a single day. If this is done, the amounts of food should be small so that more of it will be consumed. If one or two large meals are supplied, much of the food will end up as debris on the bottom of your tanks. You should also strive to vary the *kinds* of food given to your Guppies on

Nicely matched blue deltatail Guppies congregating in anticipation of being fed. Providing a good diet is the single most important element in Guppy development over which the hobbyist has complete control.

such a large diet. You should set up a rotation of brine shrimp for one feeding, flake food the next, etc. Guppies kept on the same food will not grow into fine, prize-winning fish. In fact, a steady diet of the same variety of food will cause the fish to grow up as an inferior specimen. Such fish may be susceptible to disease and will not be good breeders. A varied diet will also keep your Guppies from suffering from some forms of malnutrition. No single Guppy food contains the full requirement of the fish's nutritional needs. A wide variety aids in ensuring that nutritional requirements are more closely and more often met. Even if you have no desire to competitively breed your fish, the same diet can be boring for any variety of animal. Simple consideration should compel you to offer a variety.

Guppies 14 months or older, who are considered past their reproductive prime, should not be fed such quantities of food. If they are, they tend to grow obese. Obesity in any animal is harmful and should be avoided. These older fish should maintain a twice-a-day diet for maximum health and longer life.

If you maintain a healthy environment for your Gup-

Guppies are popular enough that fish food manufacturers formulate special foods for them alone.

Feeding a variety of foods is the key to good nutrition for Guppies. If no single food provides every needed element, using a variety of foods increases the chances for making sure that all essential elements are included in the diet, since one food might contain what another lacks.

pies and are careful about their diet, you should not encounter disease too often. Luckily, the most common reason for disease attacking Guppies is improper management of the aquarium. Fish, like humans, often suffer stress. This stress is normally caused by the fish's environment's being unsuitable or by the fact that the fish has undergone some drastic change in environment. A fish's body is usually coated with a protective coat of slime. Under healthy, normal conditions this body slime protects the fish from infection by many different disease organisms. A fish suffering stress of any kind reacts by losing some of its body slime. When the slime coating of a Guppy becomes thinner or is cast off altogether, the fish becomes very susceptible to the diseases that thrive even in healthy aquariums. These organisms will proliferate only if conditions are exactly right for them. A weakened or stressed fish is an invitation to an outbreak of disease.

As long as you are diligent about the care of your Guppies, you have conquered the main cause of disease. However,

no matter how careful you are, there is always the chance of a disease's attacking your fish. Sudden unexpected temperature changes, an undetected diseased fish with your healthy ones, a hereditary disease—all are possible reasons for ailments. You should be familiar with some of the more common diseases so that if their symptoms appear, you will know and recognize the problem. Many of these diseases can be quickly and efficiently eliminated. In some cases, although it may be a painful decision to make, it is better to destroy a diseased fish rather than trying to cure it and running the risk of infecting other fishes in the tank.

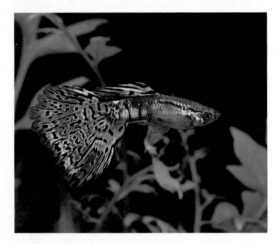

A healthy Guppy *looks* healthy. It swims constantly and non-erratically, and it holds itself erect and proudly.

The Guppy keeper should learn to recognize the general symptoms of environmental upset in his aquarium so he can stop any diseases before they break out. One sign to look for is a Guppy's gasping at the water's surface for air. This is a certain indication that the oxygen content of the water has become too low. Many times, this is due to excessive organic decomposition in the aquarium. For instance, such things as uneaten foods, dead fishes, snails, and plants can cause this condition. Organic decomposition of this kind consumes oxygen in the water and increases the amount of dissolved carbon di-

oxide. The fish are becoming asphyxiated. By making a partial water change, which will remove the source of the pollution, and by temporarily increasing the strength of aeration, you should be able to rectify this situation.

A relatively common Guppy disease is fin rot. If you notice that any of your Guppies' caudal fins become ragged along the posterior edge, then fin rot has probably set in. It is usually caused by an internal bacterial infection. This situation is dangerous. Fin rot is responsible for large populations of Guppies having to be destroyed because it was not detected and treated soon enough. After appearing on the caudal fin, the disease rapidly spreads to other fins. A short time later, the fins take on a ragged appearance and white edging appears along the ragged fin margins. Fin rot can be treated effectively by dissolving a wide-spectrum antibiotic such as Tetracycline in your aquarium water.

Worms can be a problem for your Guppies since there are many varieties that attack aquarium fishes. *Camallanus* is a red or orange intestinal roundworm or nematode that is most frequently found in the intestine of livebearers such as the Guppy. It feeds from the host's blood and its other body fluids. The worm is usually first noticed when it can be observed pro-

The tail of the half-black pastel male shown here is beginning to be consumed by fin rot; note the red at the upper portion of the rear edge of the caudal fin.

Feeding and Health

truding from the anus of the host.

Camallanus is transmitted to aquarium fishes by *Cyclops,* one of the favorite foods of Guppies in the wild. *Cyclops* are sometimes found in farm ponds, where domesticated strains of Guppies become infected.

The chemical trichlorfon is recognized as the most effective treatment against a *Camallanus* infestation. This insecticide is used by cattle farmers and wildlife managers and is sold under a number of trade names including Dylox®. Trichlorfon is carried in veterinary supply stores or farm supply stores, but usually in quantities too large to be economically sound for treating a few suffering Guppies. Your pet shop owner or a large-scale breeder may have a supply you can either borrow or

Aquarium keeping has progressed to the point that today almost every disease likely to be contracted by Guppies can quickly be remedied by easy-to-use medicines available at pet shops everywhere.

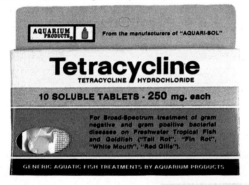

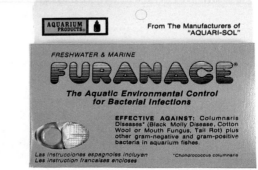

40

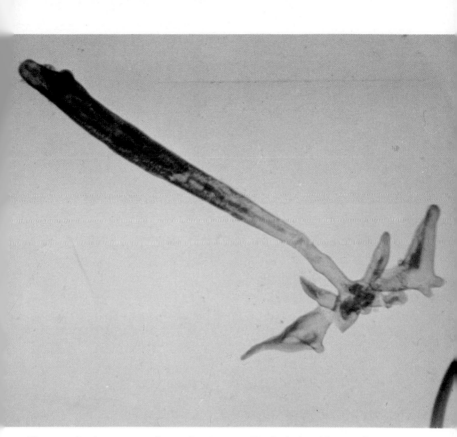

The parasite *Lernaea cyprinacea* has a worm-like look, but it's actually a crustacean.

buy. Otherwise, the hobbyist with a few tanks of Guppies can rely on several other commercial products useful in treating other varieties of intestinal worms including *Camallanus*.

Lernaea cyprinacea, the anchor worm, is another parasite which frequently attacks Guppies. It is not a worm, actually, but a modified form of a parasitic copepod. Trichlorfon is also effective in eliminating this parasitic worm.

The common disease known as Popeye or exophthalamos is also a sign of other diseases such as an internal fungal disease, bacterial kidney disease, and piscine tuberculosis, called *Ichthyophonus* (also known as *Ichthyosporidium*). This causes pockets of fluid and gas to build up behind the Guppy's eyes, causing them to bulge outward unnaturally.

One of the easiest and least expensive disease-preventive steps a Guppy enthusiast can take is simply to make regular checks on the temperature of the water—which is why owning an accurate thermometer makes good sense. The type of thermometer shown hangs on the side of the tank, but free-floating and bottom-standing thermometers (as well as digital stick-ons) are available also.

One of the most common ailments is the highly contagious white spot disease (ich) which is caused by a protozoan called *Ichthyophthirus multifiliis.* It is next to impossible to have an aquarium which does not have ich parasites present. Fortunately, they remain dormant if the Guppies are free from stress. If stress occurs, especially if it is stress caused by a sudden drastic temperature drop, a Guppy's defense against ich is lost.

If you are observing your Guppies carefully, you may discover one of the earliest symptoms of ich. Before any white spots actually appear, you will see your Guppies rubbing themselves on objects in the aquarium. A few days later, white spots begin to appear all over the infected fish. These are very small, only about the size of salt grains. The parasites have embedded themselves in the infected Guppy's skin after feeding on its body fluids for a few days. They appear as white dots after having become encysted. These cysts start to drop off the host after a few days, but additional parasites begin to form simultaneously. The cysts drop to the bottom of the tank and, inside, the protozoan begins to multiply by division. After a few more

days, the cyst breaks open, releasing new free-swimming parasites. As many as 500 of these will swim around your aquarium seeking a host. This free-swimming stage is the only one in which the ich parasites become vulnerable to the recognized standard treatment. The free-swimming stage lasts only a day, but treatment must be continued for at least ten days in order to destroy all of the parasites.

Fortunately, treating ich is easy unless the infestation has progressed past the point of no return. Pet shops sell many different ich remedies, and all are very effective if the directions for their use are followed carefully. Ich remedies often are used in conjunction with an increase in the temperature of the tank water to 80 to 85, as the parasite can't live in water that warm over a protracted period.

Another protozoan (called *Oodinium*) is responsible for the disease known as Velvet. Its name is derived from the fact that these parasitic cysts show up on the Guppies' bodies as a velvety golden coating. The *Oodinium* cysts are a great deal smaller than ich. They are harder to detect, but treatment and initial symptoms are about the same as ich. Velvet is, however,

Cysts of the protozoan parasite *Oodinium limneticum.*

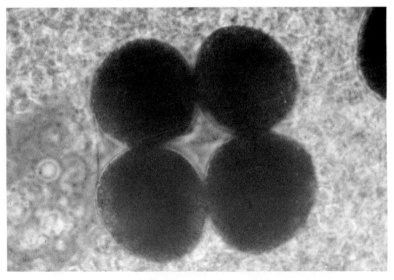

not as severe. Since *Oodinium* parasites do not respond to heat treatment as readily as do ich parasites, the treatment is a bit different. As with ich, good commercial remedies are available.

The most effective ways of eliminating diseases before they strike your guppies are the partial water changes which are part of normal aquarium maintenance. The causes of such diseases as fin rot, velvet, ich, and others are almost always present. Healthy Guppies have a far better chance of developing normal resistance than those fish which are forced to dwell in an inadequate environment. The latter also develop poor overall health which greatly lowers their natural resistance to these diseases. Changing the water on a regular schedule aids in diluting such things as plant wastes. It won't completely destroy them, but it will keep these pollutants from becoming a dangerous concentration of disease organisms.

Experienced Guppy breeders and keepers attain success in curing their fish since they have all of the necessary equipment and medications on hand. They easily overcome any delay which can often allow the disease to spread. If you are

Making regular frequent partial changes of the water in which they live is one of the best ways to keep Guppies healthy; equipment is available to allow hobbyists to make such changes effortlessly.

FACING PAGE: Nicely matched red delta males bred by Stan Shubel; these are young fish, shown shortly before beginning their show careers.

not so completely prepared by the time you discover which medication is needed, the delay may have allowed the disease to spread to other Guppies. If spreading grows to great proportions, a normal dosage of the chosen medication may not be effective. Experts caution beginners not to hurry a cure from any disease's specific time cycle. The application of more than any recommended dosage may not hasten the cure. In fact, it can be dangerous to use larger than prescribed dosages. Many medications contain ingredients that are helpful to the fish if used as prescribed, but lethal if larger quantities are used. The same is true with the use of two or more medications simultaneously. Their desired effects can sometimes cancel each other out or they can blend or mix together, often to the detriment of the fish. Drugs' effects when used together may change completely from the effects they are supposed to produce separately; the result can be lethal to your Guppies.

Nothing is more disappointing to a serious Guppy breeder than to have the development of a new strain endangered by disease. Any sort of medical disorder should be dealt with immediately to the best of your ability. If you've become familiar with the more common diseases, you will know which are contagious. If the disease in your aquarium is contagious, you will have to remove *all* of the fish at once and place them in your isolation tanks. Those Guppies which have already shown visible signs of the disease should be placed in one tank and those unaffected or presently free of symptoms in another one. The original, infected aquarium should be stripped down completely. A strong saline solution should be used to sterilize the sand or gravel for the next 24 hours. After this, these items should be thoroughly rinsed just as you would prior to initially placing them in your tank. There are many commercial sterilizing solutions for this operation (such as methylene blue) available in your local pet shop.

Virtually all non-organic materials such as plastic plants, filters, heaters, and thermometers can remain in the

FACING PAGE:
Two half-black males of different colors. These Guppies
are of strains being maintained in eastern Europe.

46

tank for sterilization. However, some commercial disinfectants will permanently discolor these items. An alternative is to remove the gravel and boil it in water, while the tank and the rest of its contents are sterilized with the commercial solution.

In conclusion, there are really no secrets to keeping your Guppies healthy. If you feed them properly, keep their

Plants, whether real or artificial, can form a very pleasing backdrop of greenery that enhances the appearance of every Guppy variety, regardless of basic body color. Plants are not strictly necessary, however, and some Guppy enthusiasts raise their stock in plantless tanks, using plants only in those aquariums that are mostly decorative in purpose.

aquariums as clean as possible and become educated enough to recognize diseases in their earliest stages, you will have a healthy, thriving population of Guppies for many years to come. If you are successful in all of these areas, you will help put an end to the myth that Guppies and other varieties of pet fish are short-lived.

Breeding

Breeding Guppies is not an activity for everyone. In fact, it is not our aim in this book to give readers a full course on Guppy breeding. However, it is a recognized fact that breeding these popular fish for both quantity and color is one of the main reasons they *are* so popular. We would be negligent if we did not include a chapter to at least introduce interested potential Guppy owners to some of the current expert thoughts on breeding.

Pet care, as we've stated, is an awesome responsibility, even with tiny pets such as fish. Breeding is an even larger one, simply because you have to be responsible for *raising* so many animals instead of just *caring* for them. We hope these next few pages will help the reader make up his mind about whether to just keep or to breed Guppies, or to even have them in his home at all.

The initial consideration is space. It is true that Guppies are easy to breed compared to other animals and other varieties of fish. However, if any degree of success is anticipated, then you have to have space enough in your home or apartment to accommodate the equipment needed for Guppy breeding. The secret is to start small, with a plan for expansion. Begin with the minimum, but plan ahead should your breeding operation prove successful enough to expand.

Two more aquariums, each with a capacity of 15 to 20 gallons, should be prepared for the development of the young Guppies to come. There should be one tank for each sex. Experts point out that by keeping the sexes separate from the earliest possible time allows them to be nurtured to maturity and more easily selectively bred.

FACING PAGE:
From top to bottom: gold albino male bred by Frank Chang; multicolor deltatail bred by Frank Mormino; blue/green bicolor bred by Jim Alderson.

A series of additional ten-gallon aquariums should be maintained, too, so you can separate and keep Guppies of certain desired color patterns which appear from time to time. Once these color groups are established, the breeder has set up the groundwork for selective breeding. This separation also allows for the possibility of diet experimentation to be easily conducted.

Keeping expenses and the overall health of the fish in mind, remember that each of these several tanks will have to have all the necessary equipment that you would normally have

This gold female Guppy probably is the mother of the baby that she is about to eat. Individual Guppy females vary in their tendency to eat their young, but in general well-fed Guppies will refrain from eating their fry.

for a single tank, such as proper lighting, heating, and filtering systems.

Once you have set up all your equipment, it is time to begin shopping for your first breeding Guppy. The first requirement is a virgin female neither too young nor too old. The male should be as close to the female's age as possible. Start them off on a conditioning diet of white worms, live or frozen foods, mosquito larvae, and the ever-popular brine shrimp, with a

Breeding

daily addition of high quality dry food. As with the equipment, buying food of good quality is the result of careful and educated shopping.

Observation of the activity of your Guppies at this point will show you that the very lively male is almost constantly swimming around the female in an elaborate display, spreading his fins before the female much in the manner of certain birds spreading their feathers. It may appear that copulation is apparently taking place a great many times. Guppy copulation occurs when the male touches its forward protruding copulatory fin to the female's genital region. Extensive observation of this act between mating Guppies has illustrated that fertilization of the female afterwards actually happens rarely. Successful sperm-transmitting copulation appears to require a longer union than these numerous pseudo-copulations. If all goes as planned, a fertilized Guppy female will produce a new batch of fry approximately every four weeks if kept warm. As

Sometimes genetic developments that are considered to improve a fish's appearance have bad effects on other characteristics of that fish. This male, for example, has greatly elongated ventral fins, but the modified anal fin, the gonopodium, also has been greatly elongated, and this strain can not breed normally.

many as five litters are produced as a result of a single mating.

The first sign that the female is about to give birth will be that her gravid spot (on the belly) will begin to appear darker in color. Impending birth is signified by the gravid spot growing even darker in color and beginning to move down the female's body toward her vent. At this point the female should be carefully removed and placed in the previously prepared separate aquarium stocked with large masses of floating plants.

Young Guppies usually are born head-first, emerging from their mother's genital opening in a curled position. They will uncurl almost immediately after they are born and will make their way to the surface, where their swim bladders are filled with air for the very first time. The best time to net them is when they begin nearing the surface.

As soon after birth as possible, remove the female and place her in another aquarium by herself. While well-fed Guppies do not usually feed on their own young, it is always best to play it safe. If you are well prepared, this should not be difficult at all. As for the newly delivered fry, they should be kept in the aquarium for at least a week for observation. If any of the young fish show deformities, they should be removed immediately and destroyed. An alternative is to actually feed them to larger fish.

This blue breeder female is very heavily pregnant and will soon drop her young. She has intense color to her tail, but unfortunately the color is irregularly distributed.

This Best in Show female bred by Stan Shubel was raised in a tank containing only a few other females and was over three inches long before she was bred for the first time.

It is also possible to begin determining the sexes and separating them after this initial week. Experts have developed a procedure for sexing the fry which needs some very basic and readily available materials. First you will need a two-gallon aquarium and a piece of black cardboard large enough to cover the back of the aquarium. Before covering the back, cut a round ½ inch hole in the very center of the cardboard. Place a small lamp with a frosted, 100-watt light bulb directly behind the hole. Using water from the aquarium containing the new fry, fill the two-gallon tank. Carefully remove two or three of the fry from their original tank and place them in the two-gallon "sexing tank." Wait until early evening when the room light is dim and, using a magnifying glass, carefully observe each Guppy as it swims through the beam of light. Under these specialized conditions, the gravid spot of the females can be easily detected. By the process of elimination, the Guppies displaying no gravid point are the males. Once the sex of each Guppy is determined, carefully remove each fry and place it in its segregated tank.

After four to six weeks, you should be able to see if any of the fry are displaying unusual color designs that greatly

A variegated snakeskin male bred by Jamie Magnifico. Snakeskin Guppies are among the popular show classes and are shown as both solid-color snakeskins and variegated snakeskins.

vary from the parents. If you are seriously working towards developing an unusual color strain, these Guppies should be segregated into another smaller aquarium with an approximate capacity of ten gallons. This is the recommended procedure that experts say should be followed in regard to any of the females that display slight body coloration or color spots on its fins. Among Guppy breeding enthusiasts, there is great honor bestowed on those who are able to produce a male and female strain of Guppies whose color markings are closely matched. This is why the study of the female coloration is met with so much serious observation and experimentation.

After six months, the time has come to choose a couple of females who have developed well-shaped bodies and finnage. Observe them carefully in your female fish tank and carefully remove them.Place these two females in the tank housing the male you have chosen. Lower the net in the water and al-

low the Guppies to eventually swim out on their own. Never drop them from the net into the water. To do so will cause undue stress to the shocked fish.

Starting this in-breeding process all over again will result in its being limitless as long as you remember that new broods should be kept separate from the original brood. This is very important to those breeders looking to develop a certain color strain, since no matter what color Guppies are, they are still of the same species and will breed freely with one another.

If you develop a serious interest, experts suggest acquiring new stock from sources different from where you acquired your original stock. This will make possible the potential of developing an entirely original "hybrid" Guppy. Such offspring will not appear after the first mating, but may take years of careful observation and seemingly endless experimentation on the breeder's part.

These half-black male deltatail Guppies are very well matched to each other in size, coloring and fin shape.

The body color of the upper female is very close to the grayish brown/brownish gray of the original wild Guppy female, but her dorsal and caudal fins show colors atypical of the wild female. The female in the lower photo shows the darkening at the rear of the body seen in many females of the half-black color variety.

Scientific breeding principles for all animals, including Guppies, were first laid down by Gregor Johann Mendel, an Austrian botanist and Roman Catholic priest educated at the University of Vienna. After entering the Augustine Monastery at Brno in 1843, he used the peas in the monastery garden to form the basis for all modern hybridization and heredity theory for both plants and animals. Applying these principles to fish, Guppy enthusiasts have developed the endless colorful and beautifully finned Guppies that are prized today around the world.

The main goal of many Guppy breeders is to develop a strain that can be reproduced over and over again. Some of the most famous varieties of Guppies include "wild," the Golden Guppy, the Blonde Guppy, and even the Albino Guppy. The skin of the "wild" normal gray female Guppy is, in reality, not gray at all. Small black pigment cells called melanophores make up the gray coloration visible to the naked eye. The pigment of these cells is made up of tiny melanin particles which

are dispersed around each cell's center, depending on the physiological state of the Guppy. The Guppy's eyes work as a "trigger" mechanism for these cells. For instance, if the Guppy is hovering over something light in color, the coloration of the animal becomes lighter. If it is swimming slowly over a darker area, the skin grows darker as well.

This blue deltatail male has very good color and a well shaped body, but it also has a mismatch in the dorsal fin color and therefore should not be used as a breeder.

The Golden Guppy appears lighter in color because it has about 50% fewer melanin particles in each of its melanopore cells. There is no known way to chemically remove these pigment cells. The appearance of the Golden Guppy is considered a *mutation* or a "jump" in the evolutionary process of an

animal. Once such mutants appear in an animal strain, genetic and heredity experts can use the mutant to begin different varieties of animals through selective and cross breeding.

The Blonde Guppy has almost as many melanophore cells as its "wild" ancestors, but the black pigment particles are much smaller in size. The Blonde Guppies appear even lighter than the Golden Guppies.

Those Guppies appearing with no pigment at all are Albino Guppies. They also appear to have pink eyes, but in reality, the eyes have no coloration at all. The pinkish color is a reflection of blood cells behind the eyes.

Half-blacks and three-quarter-black Guppies vary in both the extent of black penetration onto the tail and body and the intensity of the black shading itself.

In order to be classed as an albino for Guppy show purposes, a fish just has to have pink or red eyes. It can show colors on the body and fins, the way these veiltail snakeskins do. The plant in the background is water sprite, *Ceratopteris thalicroides.*

Years of study and endless experimentation have led to these and other varieties. Those interested in learning more of the specific scientific details about Guppy heredity, genetics, inheritance, and breeding are urged to consult their local pet shops and libraries. The endless fascination that is possible by breeding and raising fancy Guppies has helped add to the tremendous popularity of these fish in aquariums all around the world.

Breeding is a fascinating and wondrous aspect of the Guppy since it is accomplished with relative ease. Whether you are doing it for quantity or quality, the enjoyment these little fish provide is almost without limit. The Guppy may be a small fish, but he is a mighty one if you measure his hardiness, his beauty, and his worldwide popularity.

No matter how good the stock you start off with, you can't keep a good strain going unless you feed your fish well and provide them with uncrowded tanks and good water conditions—and you also have to cull systematically to weed out bad breeding stock. One of the very best ways of learning how to keep your Guppies properly and how to evaluate them for breeding purposes is to join a local Guppy club and attend Guppy shows. Specialist organizations such as the International Fancy Guppy Association do much good educational and promotional work on the Guppy scene, and its affiliated local clubs welcome new members.

The following books by T.F.H. Publications are available at pet shops everywhere.

Suggested Reading

GUPPY HANDBOOK
By Dr. C.W. Emmens
ISBN 0-87666-084-7
T.F.H. PS-668
Contents: Maintenance. Water Quality. Reproduction Of Guppies. Feeding Guppies. Raising the Young. Keeping Guppies Healthy. Guppy Genetics. Selection with Minimal Inbreeding. Reversion To or Towards Type. Color Testing in the Female. Standards for Guppies. Strains of Guppies. Prize-Winning Guppies.
Soft cover, 5½ x 8", 128 pages.
31 black and white photos, 63 color photos.

HOW TO RAISE SHOW GUPPIES
By Lou Wasserman
ISBN 0-87666-153-2
TFH PS-738
Contents: The Gratification of a Guppy Hobbyist. Equipment. Water. Feeding. A Typical Day. Maintaining a Strain. Preparation for Showing. The Show Itself. History of the Modern Day Guppy. Judging Standards.
Highly illustrated in both color and black and white, includes color photos of guppy varieties never before published.
Soft cover, 5½ x 8", 96 pages.

LIVEBEARING AQUARIUM FISHES
By Manfred Brembach
ISBN 0-86622-101-8
TFH PS-832
Contents: What are Livebearers, Keeping Livebearers, Breeding Livebearing Aquarium Fishes, Nutrition, The Mechanics of Livebearing, Behavior of Livebearers, Family Poeciliidae-Typical Livebearers, Family Goodeidae, Family Hemiramphidae-Halfbeaks, Family Jenynsiidae, Family Anablepidae.

Index